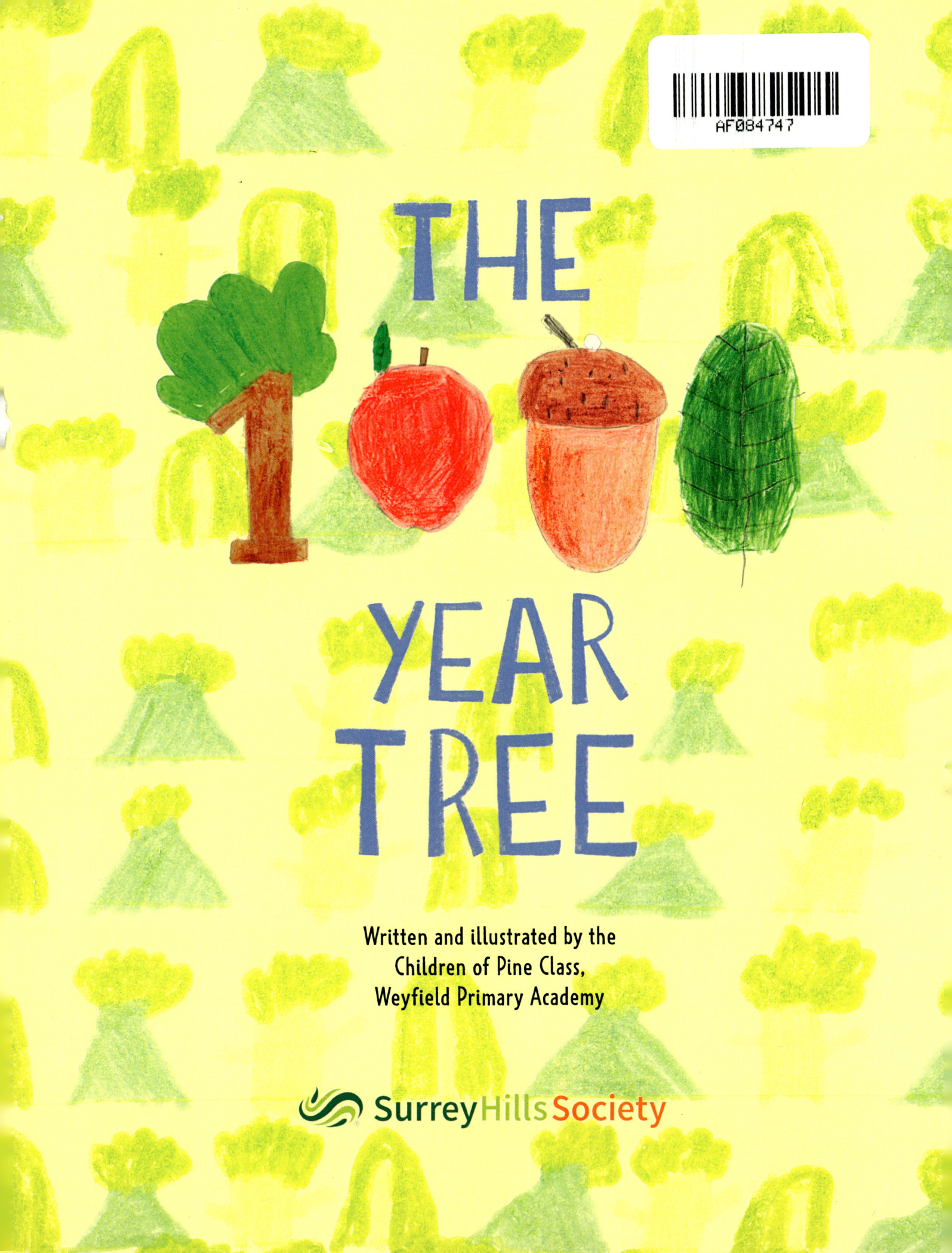

The illustrations and poems for
The Thousand Year Tree have been created
by the children of Pine Class,
Weyfield Primary Academy Guildford.

The children visited and researched the
thousand year old yew trees at Newlands
Corner, Surrey, then brought their magic
to life on the page.

The book represents a creative collaboration
led by the Surrey Hills Society to celebrate
our vital ancient trees and how we can all
protect them for the future.

Illustration by Chloe Sadlowski age 10

High on the hill, I'm a precious, ancient tree.
I've stood here for a thousand years,
Watching summers cool to autumn, winters melt to spring,
Kings and queens, badgers and deer, laughter and tears -
You wouldn't believe the things I've seen...

1024 - 1124

I saw the first battle at Hastings as I fell to the earth as a seed.

Many strange new people arrived and I watched them explore the wild landscape around my growing sprout.

Zane

1028

VIKING WARRIOR, KING CANUTE, RULES OVER ENGLAND, DENMARK AND NORWAY

CHINESE ARTISAN, BI SHENG, INVENTS CERAMIC MOVEABLE TYPE PRINTING

1041

1066

THE BATTLE OF HASTINGS MARKS THE BEGINNING OF THE NORMAN CONQUEST OF ENGLAND

My baby roots pushed through the soil.
I felt the ground shake around them
with the footsteps of wild wolves and a
Conqueror called William.

I smelt the damp soil as it splashed
against me in their wake.

lfti

**GUILDFORD CASTLE IS BUILT BY
WILLIAM THE CONQUEROR**

1085-1100

THE UNIVERSITY OF BOLOGNA IS
ESTABLISHED AS THE FIRST UNIVERSITY
IN THE WORLD

1085

THE DOMESDAY BOOK IS CREATED – A PUBLIC
RECORD OF ALL THE TOWNS VILLAGES AND
PEOPLE LIVING IN ENGLAND

1088

1119

THE KNIGHTS TEMPLAR ARE FOUNDED
TO PROTECT CHRISTIAN PILGRIMS
IN JERUSALEM

1124 - 1224

I watched men charge towards their opponents on horseback,
Their powerful hooves shaking my glossy leaves.

While lightning darted overhead, I could hear laughing voices
Dance around the crowded banquet table.

Teddy and Logan

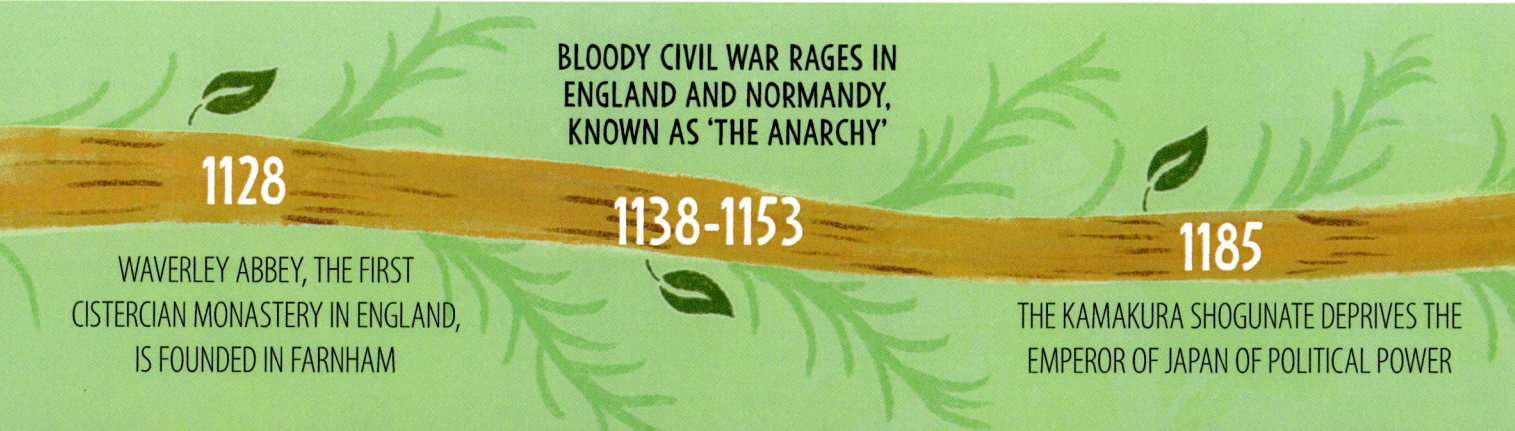

1128

WAVERLEY ABBEY, THE FIRST
CISTERCIAN MONASTERY IN ENGLAND,
IS FOUNDED IN FARNHAM

**BLOODY CIVIL WAR RAGES IN
ENGLAND AND NORMANDY,
KNOWN AS 'THE ANARCHY'**

1138-1153

1185

THE KAMAKURA SHOGUNATE DEPRIVES THE
EMPEROR OF JAPAN OF POLITICAL POWER

Poor souls darted through the King's woods
As my slender sapling reached to snatch them.

I could feel the sun's rays warming my growing trunk
As it lazily spun around the sky.

Michael and Kinley

THE KINGDOM OF ZIMBABWE BEGINS

1215

1220

1222

THE MAGNA CARTA IS RELUCTANTLY SIGNED BY KING JOHN IN A MEADOW AT RUNNYMEADE, SURREY, ESTABLISHING THE IDEA OF 'LAW' AND MEANING KINGS ARE NOT ABOVE THE LAW

ONE THIRD OF THE LAND IN SOUTHERN ENGLAND IS DESIGNATED AS 'ROYAL FOREST' - HUNTING AREAS RESERVED ONLY FOR THE KING

1224 - 1324

As the hot, dry spring covered my stem,
my blossoms started to bloom
around the churches
leading to the river.
I watched the daffodils and bluebells
rise and dust the air with pollen.

Lola

1224-1324

HUNDREDS OF MEDIEVAL MONASTERIES AND CHURCHES ARE BUILT

THE 'TREATY OF YORK' ESTABLISHES A BORDER BETWEEN SCOTLAND AND ENGLAND

1237

1240

GLASSMAKERS IN CHIDDINGFOLD, SURREY, ARE ASKED TO MAKE COLOURED GLASS FOR THE WINDOWS AT THE NEW WESTMINSTER ABBEY

All around me, I saw people suffer
and endlessly search for food.
My red berries were ripening,
but I could feel them feeding the
pecking blackbirds and thrushes.

Their movement stirred the summer
flowers that filled the breeze.

Thomas and Luke

THE MAMLUK DYNASTY IS
FOUNDED IN EGYPT

1250

1270

ENGLAND MOVES FROM BARTERING
TO A MONEY-BASED ECONOMY

1315-1317

BAD WEATHER CAUSES CROPS TO FAIL -
THE GREAT FAMINE KILLS MILLIONS OF
PEOPLE IN ENGLAND AND EUROPE

1324 - 1424

I could see people grow ill from a mysterious plague.
My branches wound higher through the coughing, crowded streets
Where I could hear the buzz of insects
And clattering carts.

Maycie-Lou and Chloe

ENGLISH BEGINS TO REPLACE FRENCH AS THE
OFFICIAL LANGUAGE OF ENGLAND

1347-1351

1362

1368

**THE BLACK DEATH KILLS A
THIRD OF THE POPULATION
OF EUROPE**

THE BEGINNING OF THE MING DYNASTY IN CHINA

I watched the longbows stretch and send their
arrows across the wide battlefield.
I fed off the soldiers' strength
As I felt my trunk grow wider and stronger,
Like the tall wheat fields around me.

Noel

GEOFFREY CHAUCER WRITES
'THE CANTERBURY TALES'

1387-1400

1408

SURREY 'WHITEWARE' POTTTERY IS PRODUCED FROM
KILNS IN CHEAM AND KINGSTON-UPON-THAMES AND
USED WIDELY ACROSS LONDON

ENGLAND WINS A DECISIVE VICTORY
OVER THE FRENCH AT THE BATTLE OF
AGINCOURT, LED BY HENRY V

1415

1424 - 1524

I could see birds flying high in the
midsummer breeze
Over the land where white roses
charged against red.

I could feel my bark thickening and
dormice running along its deeper grooves.

Crimson leaves swirled around me
and rustled in the wind
Towards the emptying crop fields.

Josh

**THE 'WAR OF THE ROSES'
BETWEEN THE LANCASTERS
AND THE YORKS**

1455-1487

1478

THE SPANISH INQUISITION
BEGINS

1431

JOAN OF ARC IS BURNED AT THE
STAKE ON ACCUSATIONS OF HERESY

While Henry's wives lost their heads,
My berries ripened and burst to the ground.

I saw their drops of scarlet, blood-bright
on the cold white snow.

Caleb and Freddie

CHRISTOPHER COLUMBUS LANDS IN
THE AMERICAS FROM SPAIN

THE CLOTH TRADE IS GROWING FAST IN GUILDFORD,
GODALMING AND FARNHAM. COULD SOME OF THIS CLOTH
HAVE BEEN USED FOR HENRY VIII'S ROBES?

1492

1509

1515

HENRY VIII IS CROWNED
KING OF ENGLAND

1524 - 1624

A little boy became King
While I grew five hundred rings,
And dormice hung off my long branches.

Olivia

KING HENRY VIII DINES AT WEST HORSLEY PLACE, SURREY. HE FEASTED ON A 35 COURSE LUNCH OF STEWED SPARROWS, LARDED PHEASANTS, GULLS, STORK AND HERON

1536

1547

EDWARD VI BECOMES KING, AGED JUST 9!

ELIZABETH I IS CROWNED QUEEN OF ENGLAND

1558

My roots reached deeper into the earth.
I could feel them stretching further through the dry land
In search of precious water.

Yannic and Abbybella

WILLIAM SHAKESPEARE WRITES SOME OF THE
GREATEST WORKS IN THE ENGLISH LANGUAGE

THE FLUSHING TOILET IS INVENTED

1585-1616

1593

1596

1605

GALILEO GALIEI INVENTS THE THERMOMETER

GUY FAWKES'S TREASONOUS
GUNPOWDER PLOT IS DISCOVERED

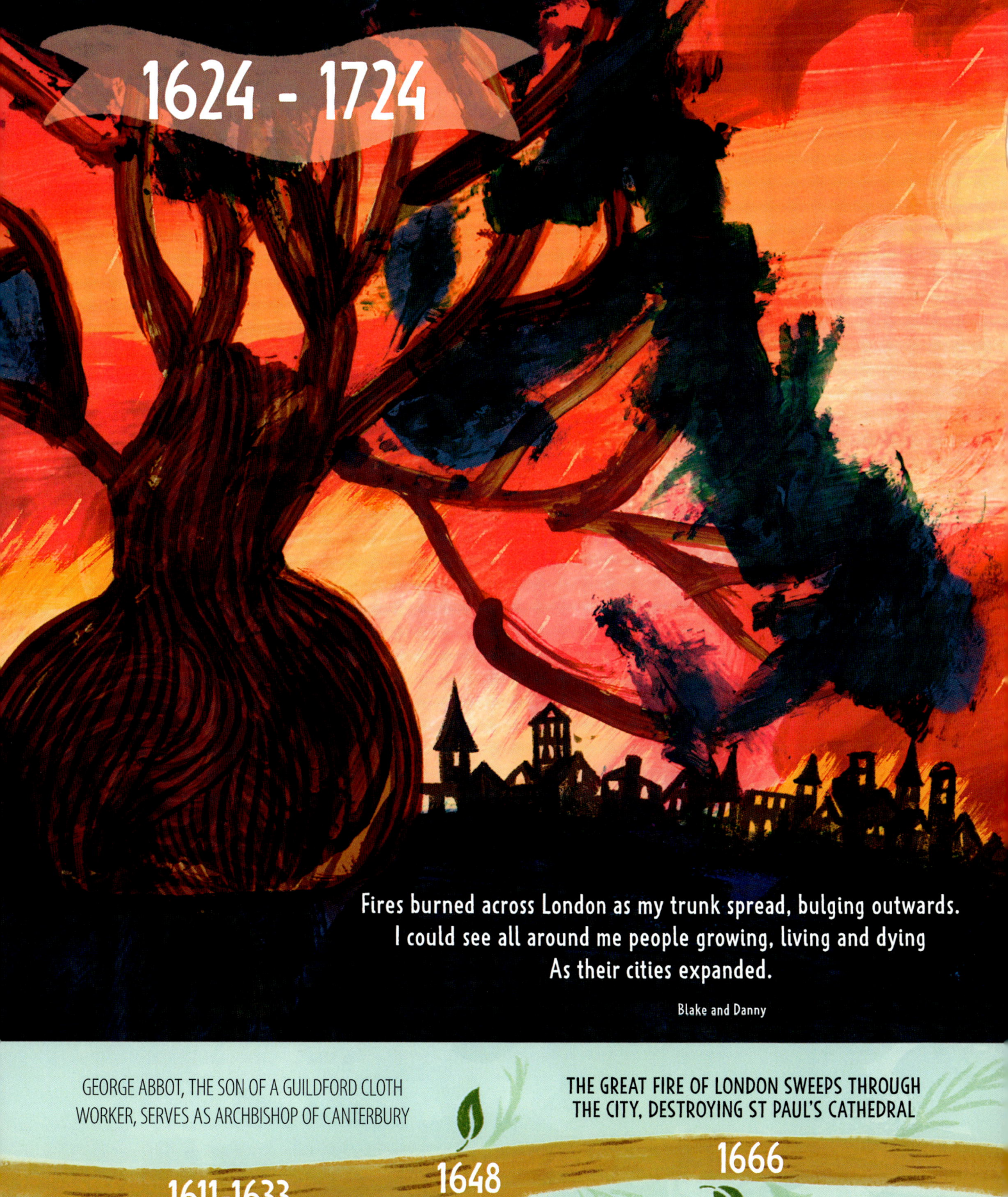

1624 - 1724

Fires burned across London as my trunk spread, bulging outwards.
I could see all around me people growing, living and dying
As their cities expanded.

Blake and Danny

GEORGE ABBOT, THE SON OF A GUILDFORD CLOTH
WORKER, SERVES AS ARCHBISHOP OF CANTERBURY

THE GREAT FIRE OF LONDON SWEEPS THROUGH
THE CITY, DESTROYING ST PAUL'S CATHEDRAL

1611-1633

1648

1666

THE TAJ MAHAL IS BUILT BY EMPEROR
SHAH JANAN IN MEMORY OF HIS WIFE

Jonathan Swift wrote a magical journey
While my branches began to shrivel with age.

I felt many small mouths nibble the plants
around my decaying trunk.

Amy and Reonie

GREAT BRITAIN IS FORMED

JONATHAN SWIFT WRITES
'GULLIVERS TRAVELS

1707

1709

1726

SURREY'S MILLS ARE THE MAIN PRODUCERS
OF GUNPOWDER IN ENGLAND

THE GREAT FROST MARKS THE
COLDEST WINTER FOR 500 YEARS

1724 - 1824

The sky was grey with smoke as shots blasted between ships.

Buildings were demolished and rose around me as I felt my crumbling bark begin to peel away.

I still saw people taking shelter from the foggy air under my shade And heard their whispered secrets.

Paddy

THE INDUSTRIAL REVOLUTION BEGINS! BIG FACTORIES START TO REPLACE TRADITIONAL COTTAGE INDUSTRY

1730

1760

1724

SAMUEL JOHNSON'S DICTIONARY OF THE ENGLISH LANGUAGE IS FIRST PUBLISHED

THE 18TH CENTURY ROYAL NAVY IS THE MOST EFFECTIVE FIGHTING FORCE IN THE WORLD

My needles grew brown and dropped with age

As the sharp guillotine fell again and again.

Later, I could feel peace growing
As many walked free under my wise branches.

Dennis

THE FRENCH REVOLUTION RAGES,
SYMBOLISED BY THE DEADLY
GUILLOTINE

THE SURREY IRON RAILWAY IS THE FIRST PUBLIC
RAILWAY SANCTIONED BY THE BRITISH PARLIAMENT

1789-1799

1800

1801

1814

FRENCH SILK WEAVER J.M.JACQUARD
INVENTS THE JACQUARD LOOM

JOSEPH NICÉPHORE NIÉPCE TAKES THE FIRST
PHOTOGRAPH USING THE CAMERA OBSCURA

1824 – 1924

While Queen Victoria was getting married,
I grew above the alleys and could see all around me.

I felt the people stepping on my roots.
I could hear the cows mooing and the sheep bleating.

I could taste the factory pollution on the air.
I felt the pain from lightning strikes hitting me.

Charlie

QUEEN VICTORIA REIGNS
AS MONARCH OF ENGLAND

JOSEPH LISTER INVENTS
ANTISEPTIC PROCEDURES

1812-1870

1867   **1876**

1833   **1837-1901**

CHARLES DICKENS WRITES BRITISH
CLASSICS INCLUDING 'OLIVER TWIST'

ALEXANDER GRAHAM BELL
INVENTS THE TELEPHONE

SLAVERY IS ABOLISHED

The unsinkable ship was swallowed by the Atlantic,
While new buds began to bloom from my fallen branches.

I saw many slip into sleep under my shade.
I heard their deep breaths and
wished them pleasant dreams.

Joey and Mason

GODALMING IS THE FIRST TOWN IN THE WORLD TO
HAVE A PUBLIC ELECTRICITY SUPPLY, PROVIDING
ELECTRIC LIGHTING BOTH IN HOUSES AND STREETS

GOTTLIEB DAIMLER BUILDS THE
WORLD'S FIRST FOUR-WHEELED
AUTOMOBILE

TWENTY MILLION FROM OVER
THIRTY NATIONS DIE IN WW1

1881   **1886**   **1912**   **1914-1918**

1886

JOHN PEMBERTON INTRODUCES
THE WORLD TO COCA-COLA

THE TITANIC SINKS AFTER STRIKING
AN ICEBERG ON ITS MAIDEN VOYAGE
FROM SOUTHAMPTON TO NEW YORK

1924 - 1974

The smell of fresh grass overwhelmed me.

I reflected on how the land used to be full of deep trenches and men running through them.

WOMEN OVER THE AGE OF 21 ARE GIVEN EQUAL VOTING RIGHTS

WINSTON CHURCHILL IS PRIME MINISTER, LEADING BRITAIN THROUGH WW2

1928

1939-1945

1940-1945

50 MILLION DIE IN WW2, THE BLOODIEST CONFLICT IN HISTORY

MAN-MADE TUNNELS FROM THE MEDIEVAL CASTLE AT REIGATE ARE USED AS AIR RAID SHELTERS DURING WW2

The bombs rained down and nearly landed
on my strong, wide trunk.

I saw the moon shining in the sky
And imagined that brave man taking his first
steps on its bright surface.

Lauren and Ava

THE SURREY HILLS NATIONAL LANDSCAPE IS
DESIGNATED AS AN AREA OF OUTSTANDING
NATURAL BEAUTY

THE FIRST MAN LANDS ON THE
MOON FROM AMERICA'S SPACE
FLIGHT, APOLLO 11

1958 1960 1969

THE WORLD IS INTRODUCED TO
THE MUSIC OF THE BEATLES

AMAZING TREES!

Did You Know?

A mature tree can support 2,300 species of wild creatures.

Trees are connected by an underground network of mycorrhizal fungi, used for sharing information and nutrients. It's like the trees have their own phoneline to each other!

All parts of a yew tree are poisonous to humans. However, yew tree leaves and berries are eaten by dormice, deer, birds and caterpillars.

Fossil records show that yew trees were growing 200 million years ago.

The drooping branches of an old yew tree can root and form new trunks where they touch the ground.

We often think that trees and their roots are tough and strong. But in fact they're easily damaged.

Humans are taking water from underground aquifers, making it harder for trees' roots to reach the water they need.

The most fragile part of a tree is the upper surface of its soil, around the tree trunk and out to at least three metres beyond the edge of the tree's canopy. Trampling on this soil compacts it, which suffocates the tree's fine roots and mycorrhizal fungi and leads to the tree itself becoming damaged.

Add your voice to the Woodland Trust's 'Protect Our Living Legends' petition to call for better legal protection of ancient trees

Give trees plenty of space to grow big and strong and be respectful of ancient trees. Tread very lightly and keep to boardwalks or footpaths to avoid compacting their roots.

Collect acorns or seeds from around the base of trees, replant them in a suitable location and watch them grow.

BE A TREE DEFENDER!

Trees are vital but they're in trouble. We've lost 95% of our ancient trees since 1850. BUT there are lots of ways you can look after them for the future.

Save water by turning off taps, taking shorter showers and harvesting rainwater - the less water humans use, the more there is for trees to drink.

Illustration by Seren Sauls age 9

WITH HUGE THANKS TO THE FOLLOWING PARTNERS WHO HAVE HELPED BRING THIS BOOK TO LIFE:

🌿 The Weyfield Primary Academy Guildford, with special thanks to the Year 4 pupils of Pine Class, Miss Mulcahy and Miss Marcham

🌿 Author Lucy Reynolds and illustrator Katie Hickey

🌿 Gordon Jackson and Christa Emmett at The Surrey Hills Society

🌿 Amanda Wood, Jonny Lambert and Rebecca Spiers at The Old Dungate Press

🌿 Alex Andrews at the Guildford Book Festival

🌿 Caroline Price and Diane Cooper at Surrey County Council

🌿 Rob Fairbanks and Emma Cole at Surrey Hills National Landscape

🌿 Geoff Monck, Ancient Tree Specialist, 'Treecosystems'

🌿 Fifty-two Surrey Libraries teams

🌿 All the children who entered the Endpapers Competition!

This book is published by the Surrey Hills Society, which is an independent charity promoting the positive enjoyment and care of the Surrey Hills National Landscape. It has been funded by the DEFRA Access for All Fund, administered by the Surrey Hills National Landscape Board.

The Society's aims are:
CONSERVE, INSPIRE, EDUCATE, ENJOY

The Society manages conservation projects with volunteers and encourages people to explore and learn about the special qualities and distinctiveness of the Surrey Hills area. To find out more, please visit www.surreyhillssociety.org.

SurreyHills Society

Copyright © 2024 Lucy Reynolds and Katie Hickey

All rights reserved

First edition printed 2024

A catalogue record of this book is available from the British Library

ISBN 978-1-3999-9760-7

No part of this book shall be reproduced or transmitted in any forms
or by any means, electronic or mechanical, including photocopying,
recording, or by any information retrieval system without written
permission of the publisher.

Published by The Surrey Hills Society

www.surreyhillssociety.org

The historical timeline included in this book represents an
illustrative overview of events and some dates may be approximate.